ALTERNATOR
BOOKS™

ATTACK ON PEARL HARBOR

Lisa L. Owens

Lerner Publications ◆ Minneapolis

Content consultant: Eric Juhnke, Professor of History,
Briar Cliff University

Lerner Publications Company
A division of Lerner Publishing Group, Inc.
241 First Avenue North
Minneapolis, MN 55401 USA

For reading levels and more information, look up this title at
www.lernerbooks.com.

Main body text set in Aptifer Slab LT Pro Regular 11.5/18.
Typeface provided by Linotype AG.

Library of Congress Cataloging-in-Publication Data

Names: Owens, L. L., author.
Title: Attack on Pearl Harbor / Lisa L. Owens.
Description: Minneapolis : Lerner Publications, [2018] | Series: Heroes of World
    War II | Includes bibliographical references and index. | Audience: Grades
    4–6. | Audience: Ages 8–12. | Description based on print version record and
    CIP data provided by publisher; resource not viewed.
Identifiers: LCCN 2017009632 (print) | LCCN 2017010514 (ebook) |
    ISBN 9781512498165 (eb pdf) | ISBN 9781512486391 (library binding : alk.
    paper)
Subjects: LCSH: Pearl Harbor (Hawaii), Attack on, 1941—Juvenile literature.
Classification: LCC D767.92 (ebook) | LCC D767.92 .O87 2018 (print) | DDC
    940.54/26693—dc23

LC record available at https://lccn.loc.gov/2017009632

Manufactured in the United States of America
1-43463-33203-6/15/2017

TABLE OF CONTENTS

INTRODUCTION
"BOMBED!"

"BOMBED! 8:00 in the morning. Unknown attacker so far! Pearl Harbor in flames!" wrote seventeen-year-old Ginger in her diary. The morning of December 7, 1941, had begun quietly, like most Sundays on the island of Oahu, Hawaii. But at 7:55 a.m., all normal activities stopped. That's when a Japanese **dive-bomber** arrived at the US military base at Pearl Harbor. It dropped a bomb on the battleship USS *Arizona* and flew up and away as quickly as it had rushed in. Pearl Harbor was under siege.

The next two hours brought a steady stream of 353 Japanese planes bombing and raining gunfire on the island. Japan's attack force also included more than sixty sea vessels such as submarines, destroyers, and battleships.

This terrifying attack killed more than twenty-four hundred Americans and wounded another one thousand, including military personnel and **civilians** of all ages. It also damaged or destroyed ships, aircraft, and homes.

The USS *Arizona* burns and begins to sink after being bombed on December 7, 1941.

5

WORLD AT WAR

World War II (1939–1945) had begun two years earlier when Germany invaded Poland on September 1, 1939. Soon after, Great Britain and France, two of the countries known as the Allied powers, declared war on Germany and its **allies**, known as the Axis powers. Japan joined the Axis powers in 1940.

Invading German forces destroyed a road in Poland early in 1939.

A Japanese fighter aircraft used in the attacks on Pearl Harbor

Japan had been working to expand its power across Asia. While the United States was trying to stop Japan, it limited Japan's access to resources such as oil. So Japan planned to take these resources from British and American territories in Asia. But first, Japan had to make sure the United States couldn't stop its plans. US military forces had been training in case the United States decided to enter World War II. But Japan was about to make that decision for the United States.

CHAPTER 1
CALM BEFORE THE STORM

Army nurse Revella Guest loved life in Hawaii. She and her friends worked hard and enjoyed parties and dances on their nights off. Guest knew that the United States might join World War II. But to most people living in Hawaii, the war seemed far away. On December 6, 1941, Guest returned home early after a dinner with her friends. She never could have imagined what the next morning would bring.

Pearl Harbor before the attack

The Japanese used a device known as the Purple Machine to encode messages during World War II. American code breakers figured out the code and were able to read many Japanese messages.

KEEPING WATCH

Meanwhile, the US government kept a close eye on the war. The government studied the battles raging in Europe and tracked Japan's movements. The US government was concerned about US–Japanese relations. But as of December 6, the United States and Japan were still discussing how to keep the peace.

People in the military kept watch too. On December 6, an American **cryptologist** decoded secret messages from Japan. The Japanese were discussing US battleship positions at Pearl Harbor. The cryptologist

thought it might be important, but her boss said he would look at it on Monday.

THE ENEMY APPROACHES

At 3:42 a.m. on Sunday, December 7, Ensign R. C. McCloy was on patrol duty on the USS *Condor*. He saw a **periscope** poking above the water less than

2 miles (3.2 km) from the harbor entrance. American submarines were not allowed to be in that area. The USS *Ward* was in a better position to investigate, so the *Condor* alerted the *Ward* of the periscope. But the *Ward* did not find a Japanese submarine until 6:45 a.m. The *Ward's* **skipper** reported the submarine, but the commander of the US fleet decided not to take immediate action.

At 7:02 a.m., military personnel at the Opana Point radar station, about 30 miles (48 km) from Pearl Harbor, noticed that blips on the radar that stood for aircraft were getting larger. That meant planes were flying toward Pearl Harbor. But officers in charge of the station assumed they were the US Air Force's B-17s, which were scheduled to arrive from California.

STEM HIGHLIGHT

Radar senses faraway objects by sending radio waves and timing how long it takes the waves to return after bouncing off an object. During World War II, radar was used to detect enemy ships and planes before they reached their targets. It was brand-new technology then, and servicemen using it at Pearl Harbor were still in training. Improvements to radar would eventually help the United States and its allies win the war.

Military personnel at Pearl Harbor didn't follow through on clues about the incoming Japanese attack. Had any of these situations played out differently, the United States may have been more prepared. Instead, the attack was a surprise.

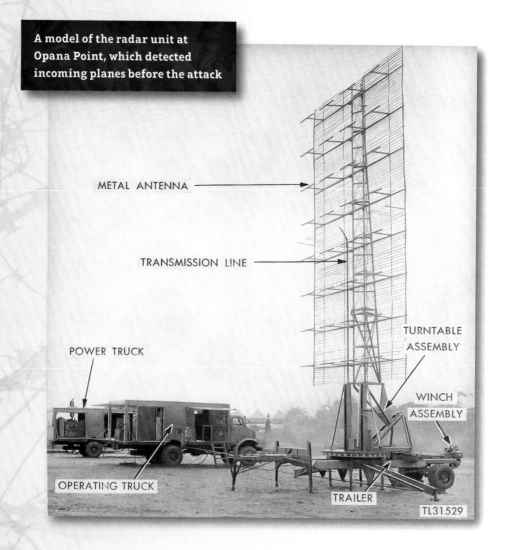

A model of the radar unit at Opana Point, which detected incoming planes before the attack

METAL ANTENNA

TRANSMISSION LINE

TURNTABLE ASSEMBLY

POWER TRUCK

WINCH ASSEMBLY

OPERATING TRUCK

TRAILER

TL31529

Pearl Harbor, 7:55 a.m., December 7, 1941

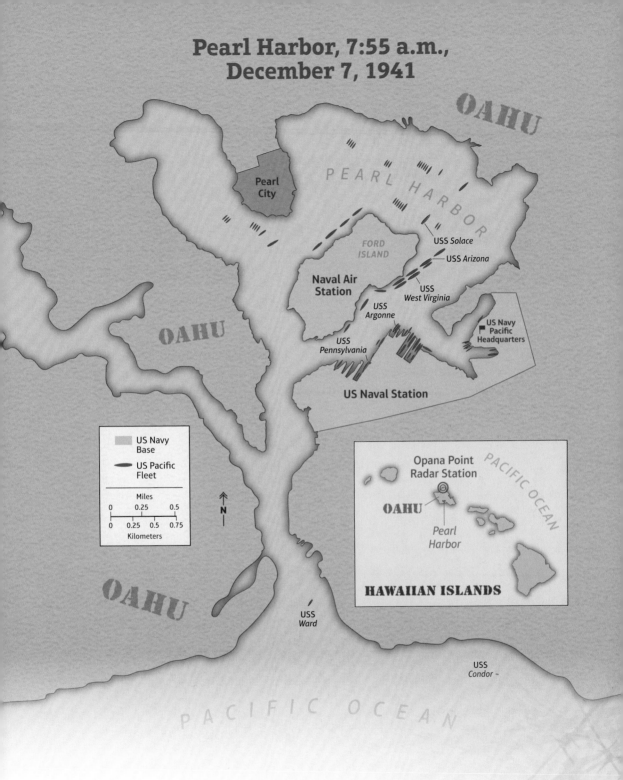

OAHU

PEARL HARBOR

Pearl City

FORD ISLAND

Naval Air Station

USS *Solace*

USS *Arizona*

USS *West Virginia*

USS *Argonne*

US Navy Pacific Headquarters

USS *Pennsylvania*

US Naval Station

OAHU

Legend

US Navy Base

US Pacific Fleet

Miles
0   0.25   0.5

0   0.25   0.5   0.75
Kilometers

N

OAHU

USS *Ward*

USS *Condor*

Opana Point Radar Station

OAHU

PACIFIC OCEAN

Pearl Harbor

HAWAIIAN ISLANDS

PACIFIC OCEAN

CHAPTER 2
MILITARY RESPONSE

Just before 8:00 a.m., sailor Warren Jones was on the USS *Argonne*. He saw a bomb strike an aircraft **hangar** on Ford Island. Jones was confused at first. "You don't know what to think then," he said. He wondered why the US forces were having a drill on a Sunday morning.

This image taken from a Japanese plane shows the beginning of the attack at Ford Island. At the time, American ships were positioned all around the island.

Admiral Husband Kimmel

But he quickly realized the truth. "It was a devastating experience," he said.

Admiral Husband Kimmel was commander in chief of the US Pacific Fleet. He saw the bombing begin and sent an urgent message to the navy ships in the area: "Air raid on Pearl Harbor! This is no drill!"

Minutes after the strike on Ford Island, fighter pilots Kenneth Taylor and George Welch jumped into Taylor's car. They were ready to fight. Still wearing tuxedo pants from a dance the night before, they were the first US pilots on the scene. They took off and shot down several enemy aircraft before their fellow American pilots were able to get into the air.

Welch (*pictured*) and Taylor both received Distinguished Service Cross awards for their actions at Pearl Harbor.

Officer John Finn was shot several times during the attack, but he did not go to the hospital for his injuries until the next day.

Officer John Finn also drove straight to his base. He grabbed a machine gun to defend against enemy fire and raced to an open field. For the next two and a half hours, he shot at every plane he saw. US forces shot down twenty-nine Japanese aircraft that day. But the surprise attack caused much greater losses for the Americans.

HERO HIGHLIGHT

Nineteen-year-old seaman Donald Stratton was at his battle station onboard the USS *Arizona* when Japan bombed the battleship. As the *Arizona* sank, he escaped with severe burns over 60 percent of his body. At the age of ninety-four, Stratton recalled: "My body was burned, my hands were raw, and I was focused on survival. I never thought about not making it." After his recovery, Stratton wanted to return to active duty to fight in honor of his 1,177 shipmates who didn't survive. One year later, he joined the Navy again.

THE PRESIDENT RESPONDS

After hearing the news from Pearl Harbor, President Franklin D. Roosevelt asked Congress to formally declare the nation's entry into World War II. Roosevelt wrote a speech on the afternoon of December 7 and addressed Congress and the nation over the radio the next day.

Millions tuned in as the president began, "Yesterday, December 7, 1941—a date which will live in infamy—the United States of America was suddenly and deliberately attacked by naval and air forces of the Empire of Japan."

By the afternoon of December 8, Congress approved Roosevelt's request to officially declare war. But as far as anyone at Pearl Harbor was concerned, the nation had joined the war at exactly 7:55 a.m. the previous day.

President Roosevelt speaks to Congress after the Pearl Harbor attack.

CHAPTER 3
QUICK THINKING

When Revella Guest reported for her shift as a nurse at the hospital early on December 7, it seemed as if it would be a typical day. But then she "heard guns and saw smoke, black smoke, coming up. . . . Then the radio started to blare that we were being attacked by the Japanese." Guest called her hospital friends to tell them to come to work. She expected **casualties**.

A Japanese plane crashed on Oahu, partially damaging a nearby hospital. The hospital continued receiving patients, and by the end of the day there were 960 casualties in the hospital.

Nurses on the USS *Solace* cared for hundreds of casualties during and after the attack. The ship did not suffer any damage.

Meanwhile, navy nurse Ann Danyo Willgrube served on the USS *Solace*, a hospital ship docked at Ford Island. The nursing staff tirelessly worked to care for the 130 wounded patients taken aboard the *Solace* during the bombing.

Willgrube was impressed by the crew of the *Solace*. She said the military had taught them the discipline they needed to carry out their duties while under attack. "We never had disaster drills," she said. "Yet when we realized that we were actually at war, every person on board that ship seemed to know instinctively what to do."

BRAVE CIVILIANS

Civilians displayed great courage that day too. As the Japanese bombed the harbor, dockyard worker George Walters had an idea. He used the crane he operated as a shield, moving it alongside the USS *Pennsylvania* to protect the ship from enemy fire. Because of the position of the ship, those on the *Pennsylvania* couldn't see enemy planes coming until it was too late. Walters

HERO HIGHLIGHT

When Japanese bombers hit the USS *West Virginia*, cook Doris (Dorie) Miller rushed to his battle station on the ship. His job was to pull injured men to safety. Many sailors were injured, and the planes were still attacking. So even though he had never had any weapons training, Miller began firing a machine gun. He thought he hit at least one enemy aircraft. Miller became the first African American to receive the Navy Cross for courage under fire.

also moved the arm of the crane to point in the direction of incoming attackers so those on the ship knew where to aim.

These clever moves put Walters at great risk. But many witnesses say that his heroism helped save the *Pennsylvania* and allowed US gunners to shoot down up to ten Japanese fighter planes.

The USS *Pennsylvania* was hit several times during the attack. It spent much of that winter under repair in California.

CHAPTER 4
AFTER THE ATTACK

By Monday, December 8, Pearl Harbor was no longer under attack. But grim reminders of the raid were everywhere. Neighborhoods were littered with wreckage. The air was thick with haze from the bombings. Oil from sinking ships was pouring into the harbor. And lifeless bodies were washing up onshore. The attack had claimed 3,581 US casualties, including 103 civilians. Nineteen US ships and 328 aircraft were

US sailors put out fires on the USS *West Virginia* following the attack. The ship had been hit by seven torpedoes.

either damaged or destroyed. People struggled to process what had happened—and what would come next.

Life on Oahu had changed. Thirteen-year-old Helen Griffith Livermont carried a gas mask and had a strict curfew. She said, "No one wanted to venture out in case the guards mistook us for the enemy!"

The United States feared another attack. And soon thousands of civilians, including families of the military personnel on the island, were evacuated to the US mainland for their own safety.

SUPPORTING THE WAR

After the attack on Pearl Harbor, the United States came together to support the war effort. Within days

Many women joined the workforce during World War II. The women pictured made oxygen masks, which were often worn by pilots.

of the United States declaring war on Japan, Germany and Italy declared war on the United States. President Roosevelt sent troops to Europe. Men and women joined the armed forces. Civilians brainstormed ways to support the troops from home. The government rationed food and raised money so there would be enough supplies for the military. Nearly everyone felt like part of the team.

In Pearl Harbor, navy crews began removing or repairing damaged and destroyed ships. Divers spent about twenty thousand hours underwater, helping with the repairs. Several ships were able to return to active duty within a few months.

STEM HIGHLIGHT

The USS *Arizona* Memorial was built over the USS *Arizona*, which sank at Pearl Harbor. Most of its crew was trapped inside. In 2013 the National Park Service started working to create a high-quality 3-D model of the ship. Divers photographed the sunken ship. Then scientists used lasers and sound waves to collect measurements and other data. One project goal is to study how the wreckage changes over time due to salt water and changing temperatures.

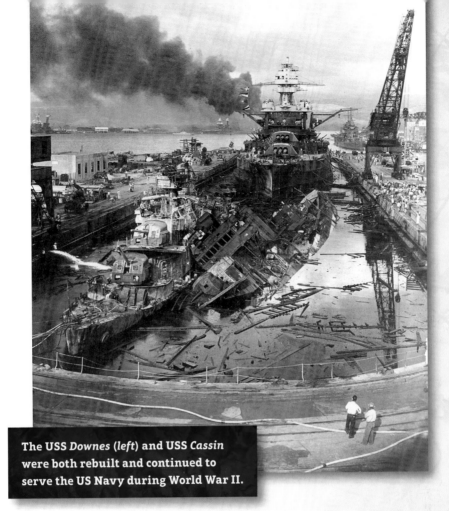

The USS *Downes* (left) and USS *Cassin* were both rebuilt and continued to serve the US Navy during World War II.

As World War II continued over the next four years, many Pearl Harbor survivors continued to serve in the military. Ray Chavez, who had been part of the USS *Condor* crew at Pearl Harbor, was one of them. In 2016, the seventy-fifth anniversary of the attack, Chavez was 104 years old, the oldest surviving veteran of Pearl Harbor. Chavez was proud to have served his country. And about the horrific day at Pearl Harbor, he said, "I hope people never forget. They can't."

Timeline

September 1, 1939	Germany invades Poland, beginning World War II.
August 1, 1941	The United States blocks Japan's access to oil.
December 6, 1941	A US cryptologist decodes a Japanese message about battleship positions in Pearl Harbor.
December 7, 1941	
3:42 a.m.	A sailor on the USS *Condor* sees an unidentified periscope in the restricted waters of Pearl Harbor.
7:02 a.m.	Japanese aircraft spotted on US radar heading toward Hawaii are mistaken for American B-17 bombers.
7:55 a.m.	The attack on Pearl Harbor begins.
8:10 a.m.	A bomb hits the USS *Arizona*, causing it to sink with more than one thousand crew members inside.
11:00 a.m.	The attack ends.

December 8, 1941	Congress approves President Roosevelt's declaration of war on Japan.
December 11, 1941	Italy and Germany declare war on the United States. The United States becomes a full participant in World War II.
September 2, 1945	World War II ends in an Allied victory.
December 7, 2016	The seventy-fifth anniversary of the attack is observed in Pearl Harbor.

Source Notes

4. "Ginger's Diary," Essential Pearl Harbor, accessed April 4, 2017, http://ospreypearlharbor.com/accounts/gingers-diary.php.

14–15. "December 7, 1941: Pearl Harbor Timeline," *National Geographic*, accessed April 4, 2017, http://www.nationalgeographic.com /pearlharbor/print.html.

15. U.S. Naval War College, "Naval College War Museum Announces New Exhibit 'This Is No Drill,'" news release, December 7, 2016, https://www.usnwc.edu/About/NWC-Museum/This-is-no-Drill.aspx.

18. Donald Stratton, "Pearl Harbor Survivor Recalls Bombers Smiling and Waving from Planes," *New York Post*, November 19, 2016.

19. "'A Date Which Will Live in Infamy': The First Typed Draft of President Franklin D. Roosevelt's War Address," National Archives, accessed April 4, 2017, https://www.archives.gov/education/lessons /day-of-infamy.

20. Robert S. La Forte and Ronald E. Marcello, *Remembering Pearl Harbor: Eyewitness Accounts by U.S. Military Men and Women* (New York: Ballantine, 1992), 235.

21. Katie Lange, "The Pearl Harbor Attack, as Remembered by the Nurses Who Were There," December 2, 2016, https://www.army.mil /article/179038/the_pearl_harbor_attack_as_remembered_by_the _nurses_who_were_there.

25. K. D. Richardson, *Reflections of Pearl Harbor: An Oral History of December 7, 1941* (Westport, CT: Praeger, 2005), 39.

27. Rose Minutaglio, "Oldest Surviving Pearl Harbor Vet to Visit Base on 75th Anniversary: 'I Hope People Never Forget,'" *People*, December 7, 2016.

Glossary

allies: countries that support one another in a military effort

casualties: people wounded or killed during war

civilians: people who aren't members of the military

cryptologist: a scientist who studies coded messages

dive-bomber: a military plane that dives directly at a target to release bombs or gunfire

hangar: a shelter for housing and repairing aircraft

periscope: an instrument with lenses and mirrors, used to see something that would otherwise be blocked. Submarines use periscopes to look above water.

skipper: the leader of a ship

Further Information

The Attack on Pearl Harbor
http://www.watchknowlearn.org/Video.aspx?VideoID=27327

Cahill, Bryon. *Freedom from Fear.* South Egremont, MA: Red Chair, 2013.

Ducksters: World War II
http://www.ducksters.com/history/world_war_ii

Garland, Sherry. *Voices of Pearl Harbor.* Gretna, LA: Pelican, 2013.

Pearl Harbor Facts for Kids
http://www.american-historama.org/1929-1945-depression-ww2-era/pearl-harbor-facts.htm

Roesler, Jill. *Eyewitness to the Bombing of Pearl Harbor.* Mankato, MN: Child's World, 2016.

INDEX

PHOTO ACKNOWLEDGMENTS

The images in this book are used with the permission of: Design: © iStockphoto.com/aaron007 (barbed wire frame); Backgrounds: © iStockphoto.com/akinshin, (barbed wire backgrounds throughout); © iStockphoto.com/ElementalImaging, (camouflage background); Mondadori Portfolio/Getty Images, pp. 4–5; Sueddeutsche Zeitung Photo/Alamy Stock Photo, p. 6; Keystone/Getty Images, p. 7; INTERFOTO/Alamy Stock Photo, p. 8; PJF Military Collection/Alamy Stock Photo, p. 9; U.S. Naval History and Heritage Command Photograph, pp. 10, 21, 23; H.W. Andrews/Wikimedia Commons (PD), p. 12; © Laura Westlund/Independent Picture Service, p. 13; The Granger Collection, New York, pp. 14, 15, Aviation History Collection/Alamy Stock Photo, p. 16; PJF Military Collection/Alamy Stock Photo, p. 17; INTERFOTO/Alamy Stock Photo, p. 19; Wikimedia Commons (PD), pp. 20, 22; Everett Collection Inc/Alamy Stock Photo, pp. 24, 25; Newscom, p. 27.

Front cover: © Universal History Archive/UIG/Getty Images; © iStockphoto.com/akinshin (barbed wire background); © iStockphoto.com/ElementalImaging (camouflage background); © iStockphoto.com/MillefloreImages (flag background).